This Book
Belongs To:

....

....

FIVE-MINUTE TALES
for
SIX
Year Olds

FIVE-MINUTE TALES
for
SIX
Year Olds

A beautiful collection of original stories

p

Illustrated by Anna C. Leplar

(Elizabeth Roy Literary Agency)

Language consultant: Betty Root

This is a Parragon book
This edition published in 2006

Parragon
Queen Street House
4 Queen Street
Bath BA1 1HE, UK

ISBN 1-40546-957-9

Printed in China

Contents

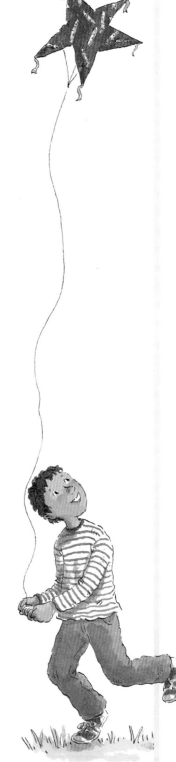

Captain Clegg and the Ship's Cat

Nicola Baxter

In the middle of the night, in the middle of the ocean, in the middle of his cabin on board the *Maisy May*, Captain Clegg lay awake. It wasn't the creaking of the timbers below that stopped him from sleeping. And it wasn't the flapping of the sails above. What was keeping the sleepless captain awake was a little scritch-scratching noise just by his left ear.

Captain Clegg rolled over and shut his eyes tightly, but he could still hear the noise. This time, it seemed to be coming from just behind his right ear.

"That's enough!" yelled Captain Clegg. "Ow!" He sat up suddenly and banged his head on a beam. He knew that he had to do something about the 'giant mice' on board his ship.

Now, you and I know that the animals running around sailing ships and making scritch-scratching noises are probably rats. But Captain Clegg didn't like the idea of rats aboard the *Maisy May*. It made him happier (although not much) to think of them as giant mice. It wasn't just the scritch-scratching noise that bothered him. His breakfast biscuit was often nibbled around the edges. And the ship's stores were being eaten up, too.

"As soon as we get to port," said the captain, "I'm going to buy the biggest, fattest cat I can find. That'll show 'em!"

Sure enough, the moment the *Maisy May* reached land, Captain Clegg left his ship and set off to find a cat.

The captain didn't know much about choosing cats, but he had one idea firmly fixed in his mind. To deal with giant mice, he decided, you need a giant cat.

At last, he came to a market where a thin man was selling lemons. Beside him, an enormously fat cat was sleeping in the sun.

"Lemons! Sharp and juicy!" sang the man, but the captain interrupted him.

"Never mind the lemons!" he said. "I'll give you forty pounds for your cat."

"Done!" said the thin man without a moment's hesitation. Captain Clegg picked up the enormously fat cat, tucked him under his arm and staggered back to the ship.

That night, the *Maisy May* sailed out

onto the ocean once again. Captain Clegg prepared himself for another disturbed night. After all, there was sure to be a bit of squeaking and scrabbling while the new ship's cat set to work, getting rid of the giant mice.

But the new cat simply ... slept. Well, not simply. She snored as well, pretty loudly. Between the scritch-scratching noise in his left ear and the cat's snoring in his right ear, Captain Clegg did not have a happy night. He reassured himself that the cat needed time to settle in. In the morning, he would see some action!

What he saw the next morning was a severely seasick cat. All day long the cat was either being sick or lay sleeping in her bed. So Captain Clegg had a very unhappy day, followed by another night filled with scritch-scratching noises.

When the sun came up the next morning, however, the captain was delighted to see that his new cat was bright-eyed and prowling around the cabin.

"Looking for giant mice, are you?" asked the captain.

After a day and a night of feeling seasick, the ship's cat was now looking for some breakfast – and mice were not what she had in mind. Captain Clegg watched in dismay as the cat gobbled up his entire ration of breakfast biscuits as well as lots of the ship's stores.

Over the next few weeks, Captain Clegg became more and more miserable. Not only did the cat eat all of the captain's meals, but she insisted on sleeping in the middle

of his bunk too! And she didn't catch a single mouse. At
night, lying on the deck wrapped in an old ship's flag, the
captain was too uncomfortable to sleep. He began to think
that any amount of scritch-scratching noise was better
than no bed and no breakfast. That cat would have to go.

One week later, the *Maisy May* docked in a small
port. The captain lost no time in taking his cat on shore
and selling her, although he made a considerable loss on
the deal. And the cat made her feelings known by digging
her very sharp claws into Captain Clegg's arm.

That night, Captain Clegg settled
down in his bunk once more. In the morning, he
felt extraordinarily peaceful. Not only had he slept well,
but the ship was strangely quiet. Yes, there was creaking
from the timbers below. Yes, there was yelling from the
sailors above. But there was not even the tiniest
scritch-scratching noise.

Can you guess why? The
ship's mice were so fed up
with having no breakfast
biscuits to eat (in fact
no rations of any food
at all), that they
had all jumped
ashore at the last
port. Captain
Clegg's sleep was
undisturbed ... at last.

17

The Riddle of the Tooth Fairy

Jan Payne

"Mum," said Tom, grinning up at his mother. "Look at my teeth!"

Mum looked. Instead of a complete row of small white teeth, Tom had a big gap.

"That's great!" said Mum. "It's come out at last."

Tom held out a small tooth in the palm of his hand. "What happens now?" he asked.

"Put the tooth under your pillow when you go to bed, and the tooth fairy will come and take it away."

"Pooh!" said Tom. "I don't believe in tooth fairies. That's a girly thing. James said so."

James was Tom's best friend.

"Well, it's up to you," said Mum, smiling.

That night, when he went to bed, Tom was busy thinking. He wasn't sure what to do about his tooth. There weren't any tooth fairies, he was sure about that! Well, that's what James had said. James was two months older than Tom, and better at sums, so he must be right. But then, Mum seemed to think there might be ... tooth fairies ... So, he might as well put the tooth under his pillow.

"What have I got to lose?" thought Tom. So this is what he did, and then went to sleep.

Meanwhile, the tooth fairies were having a meeting. There were three of them – Whizzy-Whiz, Star and Moonshine.

"Did you hear what Tom said?" asked Star.

"Yes, I did! Fancy not believing in us!" exclaimed Moonshine.

"He said it was girly!" shrieked Whizzy-Whiz.

"We can't have that," said Star. The other two shook their heads.

"We'll have to teach Tom a lesson," said Moonshine.

"I'm afraid so," said Whizzy-Whiz.

When Tom woke up the next morning, he looked under the pillow. His tooth had gone, and there in its place was a scrap of paper with very, very tiny writing on it!

"Mum," called Tom, running down the stairs. "Look at this!" He showed her the piece of paper. Mum read it out loud.

"Find me – you'll be richer by far,
When the Moon is bright and there's JAM on the jar.
Taste it – you'll soon be aware,
That we have been both honest and fair!"

Mum looked puzzled. "It looks like some kind of riddle," she said.

"What does it mean?" asked Tom.

"I don't really know," answered Mum.

When Tom lost another tooth, he couldn't wait to go to bed and put it under his pillow.

"I'm going to stay awake all night," he said out loud. "Then if there are tooth fairies I'll see them." And he pulled the covers up to his chin.

In just five minutes, Tom was fast asleep!

In the morning, Tom's tooth was gone and again, in its place, was a riddle. It was a different one.

"I'm brown and yellow with stripes and two wings,
There's a part of my body which is nasty and stings.
I've recently moved, now I live far away,
So my house is empty; or it was yesterday!"

"Well," said Mum, "there are more clues, this time. What is brown and yellow, with stripes and two wings?"

"A butterfly!" cried Tom, clapping his hands together in excitement.

"Good try," said Mum, "but what about the next line: 'There's a part of my body which is nasty and stings.' Butterflies don't sting."

"A wasp!" shouted Tom.

"It could be," laughed Mum. "And a wasp lives in a nest."

When another tooth came out, Tom went to bed tingling with excitement. In the morning, there was a third riddle.

"What's in the jar with JAM on the label?
Remember who makes it, if you are able.
Which is the house where they used to live?
Come tonight, we have something to give."

"Let's look at all the jars on the shelf in the cupboard," said Mum. When they looked there was one jar which just had the word 'JAM' written on its label.

"That's it! That's it!" shouted Tom, jumping up and down.

Mum opened the jar and they looked inside. Instead of jam there was honey inside the jar!

"Honey!" cried Mum. "And the riddle says, 'Remember who makes it'!"

"Bees make honey!" said Tom, clapping his hands together. "And the house where they used to live is the empty bee-hive in the garden!"

"YES!" shouted Tom, "YES! And we have to go there ... tonight!"

"You'll have to wait until it gets dark," said Mum.

That night, when the moon was shining brightly, Tom crept into the garden. Mum watched him from the kitchen door. As he moved nearer the bee-hive he could see a light coming from inside. Tom could hardly bear to look. When he did, three little voices called out,

"SURPRISE!"

There inside the bee-hive were Whizzy-Whiz, Star and Moonshine!

When they saw Tom, each fairy in turn flew around his head three times, then kissed him on the cheek and disappeared.

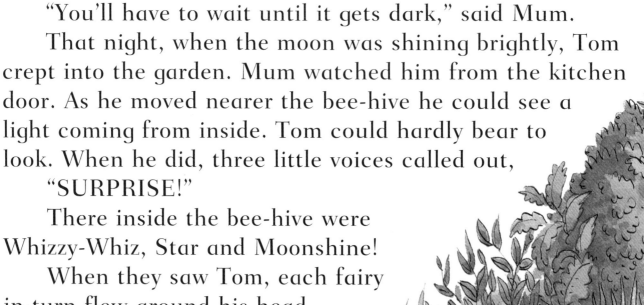

After they had gone, Tom could still hear the ringing sound of their silvery laughter.

"They've left something for you," said Mum.

There on the grass were three shiny coins – one coin for each of Tom's three teeth!

"Now what are you going to tell your friend James?" laughed Mum.

"That there are tooth fairies, of course!" replied Tom.

Sam and the Red Kite

Nick Ellsworth

It was a really blowy Saturday morning. Sam and his dad wrapped up warmly to go for a walk in the park.

Sam didn't like walking that much, but what he did like were the huge sticky buns that Dad bought in the park café.

"Come on, I'll race you to the top of the hill," shouted Dad as they went into the park.

Sam ran as hard as he could, and he just managed to overtake Dad before they reached the top.

"Hooray, I've won!" yelled Sam, as he jumped around and waved his arms.

"Wow! Look at that!" said Dad, pointing up at the sky.

The sky was full of brightly coloured kites.

There were square ones
and round ones, huge ones and tiny
ones. They were in every colour you could
think of. Some were spotty, some were stripy and
some were quite plain. Some swooped and dived like
great big birds. Others hovered in the air, as if waiting
for a gust of wind to make them dance.

Sam gazed up in wonder. Suddenly, he knew that he
wanted a kite more than anything else in the world.

"Dad, please can you buy me a kite?" he asked.

"Well, maybe for your birthday," replied Dad.

"But that's weeks away!" sighed Sam.

"Then you'll just have to wait," grinned Dad.

A few days later, Sam was out shopping with Mum. As they turned a corner, he saw a large red kite in the toyshop window. The kite was star shaped, and had tiny rockets painted all over it.

Sam thought it was the best kite he had ever seen.

"Mum, look at that!" he exclaimed, pressing his nose against the shop window. "Can I have it ... oh, please?"

"Maybe for your birthday," replied Mum.

"That's what Dad said, but my birthday's weeks away!" he groaned.

"It's something to look forward to then, isn't it?" replied Mum.

The next time they went shopping, Sam and Mum walked past the kite shop again. But to Sam's horror, the kite was no longer there. It must have been sold.

Sam was so disappointed that he decided to build his own kite. He wanted it to be just like the one in the shop.

Luckily, Mum had an old red sheet he could use. First, he found some thin bits of wood in the garden shed and glued them together in a star shape.

Then, Mum cut up the sheet into the shape of a kite.

Sam stretched it tightly over the frame, while Mum glued the sheet carefully onto the wood.

While the glue was drying, Sam ran upstairs to fetch a sticker book from his bedroom. There were no stickers of rockets in it, but there were lots of plane stickers.

Sam stuck the little planes all over the kite, making sure he didn't press too hard in case the sheet ripped.

Finally, he got a large ball of string, and tied one end onto the middle of the frame.

"There!" said Sam, looking at his finished kite proudly. Now it was time to see if it would fly!

Sam grabbed the ball of string, and started to run down the garden. Looking back, he saw that the kite was dragging along the ground.

"Fly, please fly!" he urged, running a little faster. Suddenly, a big gust of wind lifted the kite into the air.

"Look, Mum, it's flying!" cried Sam.

But, just as he spoke, another gust of wind caught the kite, and it flew straight into the branches of a tree.

"Oh no!" yelled Sam, tugging on the string to try to free it.

The kite was well and truly

stuck, so Sam tugged a little bit harder. Suddenly, the kite fell out of the tree and lay limply on the ground. The frame had broken, and the red sheet flapped noisily in the breeze. Sam was so upset, he started to cry.

"Never mind, Sam," said Mum, putting a comforting arm around his shoulder. The next morning, as Sam was getting dressed, he noticed something wrapped up at the foot of his bed. He tore off the paper, and was amazed to see the beautiful red kite from the toyshop.

"It's the red kite with the rockets!" Sam gasped. "But I thought it had been sold!"

"It had! It was Dad who bought the kite," laughed Mum, coming into Sam's bedroom. "We were going to give it to you for your birthday but, after yesterday's accident, we thought you should have it now."

"Thanks, Mum. It's the best present ever," he said, giving her a big hug.

Running into the garden, Sam held tightly onto the string. The kite rose high into the sky above him.

Sam couldn't wait to take his new kite to the park with Dad. They could watch it fly there for hours and hours. Sam knew that his kite would be the best one in the whole park – for sure!

Flying to the Moon

Nick Ellsworth

Princess Abigail was a dreamy sort of girl. Every night, she would stare out of her bedroom window looking at the moon. Abigail so wanted to visit it. Her parents, the king and queen, thought she was a very silly girl, and that she should stop dreaming. They wanted her to take more interest in her schoolwork.

Abigail's grandfather was a mad inventor, who lived by himself in a nearby tower. Abigail loved him a lot, and always looked forward to visiting him.

One day, Grandpa was showing Abigail his very latest invention – a talking teapot. Suddenly, Abigail blurted out that she had one great ambition … to go to the moon.

"How wonderful!" said Grandpa gleefully. "I've always wanted to go to the moon too! In fact," he whispered, "I've got a secret rocket that we could use to go there. All I need to make it work is the hottest mustard in the kingdom, and one long, thick hair from a black cat."

Abigail was very excited, and promised to bring her grandfather what he needed.

The next evening, when everyone was asleep, Abigail got out of bed, dressed herself and tiptoed downstairs to the palace kitchens. She took a jar of extra-hot mustard from the larder and put it in her pocket.

Then she went into the courtyard where the palace cats roamed around. After a while she spotted a beautiful black cat. She took out her scissors and cut one long hair from its thick fur.

"Thank you, puss," said Abigail, gently stroking him. "You're going to help me fly to the moon."

Getting on her favourite horse, Abigail rode out of the palace gates towards Grandpa's tower.

"Did you get everything?" Grandpa asked anxiously as he greeted her.

"I think so," replied Abigail, giving him the mustard and the cat's hair.

"Excellent!" chuckled Grandpa.

Just then, the doors of the workshop flew open, and there stood the king and queen. They looked very angry indeed.

"And what are you doing here at this time of night, Abigail?" asked the queen.

"Nothing!" replied Abigail. "I just wanted to see Grandpa."

"But it's so late!" said the king. "You two are up to something. I know you are."

The king and queen took Abigail back to the palace and told her not to visit her grandfather on her own again.

Back in her room, Abigail felt very sad. "I'll never get to the moon now," she wept.

Suddenly, a large crow appeared at her window. In its beak was a note from Grandpa, which described a secret passage behind the fireplace in her bedroom. It led all the way to Grandpa's tower! He told her to come at once, so they could leave for the moon that very night.

Abigail easily found the secret passage, and hurried along it as fast as she could. It wasn't too long before she came to a small door. She opened it, and there stood Grandpa.

"Ah, there you are!" he cried. "Are you ready? We'll be leaving in a few minutes."

"But how do we get to the rocket?" asked Abigail.

"You're standing in it," laughed Grandpa. "This whole tower is the rocket!"

Just then, Abigail looked out of the window, and noticed the torches of riders heading towards the tower.

"Oh, no," she wailed. "It's my parents. They must know I'm here!"

"Then there's no time to lose," said Grandpa, pressing a large red button on the wall.

With a terrific WHOOOSH, the tower lifted off the ground and flew high into the sky.

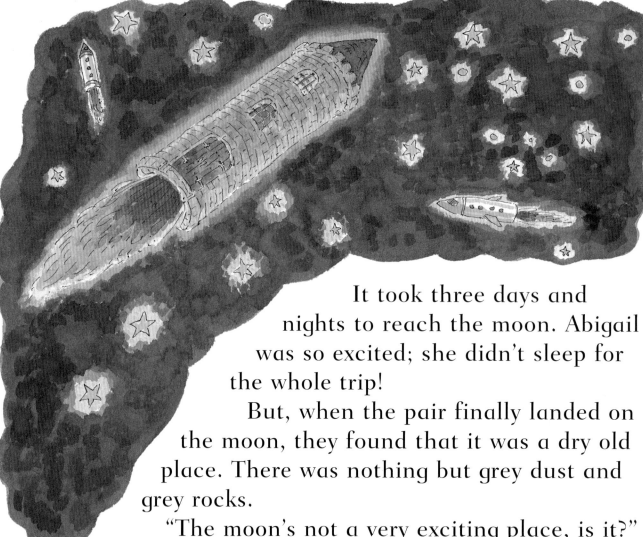

It took three days and nights to reach the moon. Abigail was so excited; she didn't sleep for the whole trip!

But, when the pair finally landed on the moon, they found that it was a dry old place. There was nothing but grey dust and grey rocks.

"The moon's not a very exciting place, is it?" said Abigail, who was starting to miss her parents.

"Can we go back, please?" she asked.

"Of course we can, my dear," said Grandpa kindly. "It's a pity the moon isn't more fun. But, at least we got here, didn't we?"

They blasted off and, three days and nights later, Abigail and Grandpa arrived safely back home.

"Hello, Mum! Hello, Dad!" cried Abigail, rushing into the arms of her parents.

"Where have you been? We've missed you so much!" cried the king and queen, hugging their daughter.

"Can Grandpa come and stay with us at the palace? Please!" asked Abigail.

"Of course he can," her parents replied. "How else can we keep an eye on him and his mad inventions?" joked the king.

"Hooray!" yelled Grandpa. "I'm going to live at the palace!"

So the king and queen, Abigail and Grandpa all lived together happily ever after.

No More Mud!

Nicola Baxter

Mr Pig felt proud when he looked at his eight piglets. "What handsome little piglets!" he smiled. "Look at those fine strong feet! Look at those little pink snouts! How they'll love rolling in the mud with their old dad. I can hardly wait!"

After only a few weeks, those little piglets had grown up so quickly – and they were into everything. They sniffed around in the straw with their little pink snouts. They explored every corner of the pigsty. They trampled in

the food trough with their fine strong feet. But, most of all, they loved playing around in the big muddy patch near the gate.

"Wheeee!" squealed the piglets, as one after another they skidded into the mud and rolled over and over. It was hard to tell them apart when they were covered from head to tail with the sticky brown mud.

"Wonderful!" snorted Mr Pig proudly. "I remember when I was a piglet …"

But the eight piglets were too busy sliding …
and splattering …
and splodging …
to listen to Mr Pig.

It was Mrs Pig who first noticed that there were only seven happy, muddy piglets playing near the gate. For a moment she couldn't work out which one was missing.

Then she squealed, "Where's Tuggle?" He certainly wasn't in the mud with the others.

A moment later, the panic was over. Tuggle was sitting peacefully in the pigsty, chewing thoughtfully on a long piece of straw.

"Aren't you feeling well?" asked Mr Pig. "Come out and play with the others!"

"Come on!" squeaked his seven brothers and sisters.

"No, thanks," said Tuggle. "I might get my feet dirty."

Mr Pig was so surprised that he could hardly speak. "But that's the idea," he spluttered at last. "Mud, my boy! Good, healthy mud! There's nothing like it for making a pig grow up big and strong – just like me!"

Tuggle shivered. "But it's messy!"

Mr Pig was becoming more and more concerned. "What's wrong with mess? You're a pig! What are little pink noses for? What are fine strong feet for?"

"My feet," said Tuggle proudly, "are pink and clean. I want to keep them that way." He stuck his snout in the air and turned his back on Mr Pig.

The other piglets had come to listen. Squelching around in the mud near the sty door, they couldn't believe their muddy little ears. Over the next few days, as they became bigger and stronger, the other piglets started to tease their brother.

"Hey, Tuggle!" the biggest piglet would yell. "Don't get muddy!" And a ball of straw soaked in the muckiest mud would come shooting across the farmyard. His aim was not good, but still Tuggle had to take cover to avoid the whizzing mud ball.

One by one, the other piglets all learned to kick. They still couldn't aim well but, when seven mud balls are rushing through the air, one of them is likely to land on a very clean piglet.

One afternoon, Tuggle cried, "That's enough!" He had spent all day dodging the flying mud balls. He decided to get away from his teasing brothers and sisters. Tuggle raced across the farmyard on his surprisingly speedy feet and made one huge leap onto the sloping roof of the pigsty. As his brothers and sisters watched in amazement, Tuggle landed on the roof with a clatter. He began to scramble upwards, well out of reach of his surprised family on the ground below.

"Ha!" squeaked Tuggle. "You can't get me now!"

But he spoke too soon. While a pig's feet are perfectly good for slipping and sliding around in the mud, they are not designed for climbing on a roof. With a loud squeal, Tuggle found himself sliding down the roof with increasing speed. There was nothing at all he could do to stop himself.

"Whoooooosh!" Down the roof he slid. "Wheeeeeeeee!" He sailed over the heads of his brothers and sisters, his astonished father and his worried mother.

"Splat!" Tuggle landed right in the middle of the biggest, muddiest puddle in the whole farmyard.

There was a terrible silence. The piglet in the puddle was completely covered in mud. The other piglets held their breath and waited for a loud yell.

Tuggle looked too shocked to speak. He shook the mud from his ears. He picked up one muddy foot and looked at it in surprise. Then the biggest smile started to spread across his face.

"It's brilliant!" cried Tuggle. "I want to do it again!" And he (and seven other excited piglets) raced across the yard and, one by one, leaped onto the pigsty roof and began climbing.

"Oh, no!" cried Mrs Pig. But what do you think she and Mr Pig could do about their leaping piglets? Absolutely nothing!

Ben Has a Good Idea

Nick Ellsworth

Ben and his parents had just moved into a new house. It had a very large garden, which gave Ben a lot of space to kick his football around. Ben loved football. He was a great fan of his local team, and watched all their matches when they were on television.

While his parents were busy unpacking, Ben wandered into the garden to play with his football. He put the ball down on the grass, and imagined he was taking a penalty shot for his team.

Ben took a bit of a run, and kicked the ball as hard as he could.

"GOAL!!" cried Ben, flinging his arms into the air. But it wasn't a goal at all. The ball rose high in the air, and then sailed slowly over the wall into the garden next door.

"Uh oh," thought Ben. "I hope I haven't broken anything."

He peered over the wall, and was astonished to see that on the other side was a wonderful garden. There were plants and flowers of every shape, size and colour. A summerhouse stood at one end of the garden, and in the middle of the perfect lawn there was a small pond with a little bridge over it.

Ben suddenly noticed an old man digging in one of the colourful flower-beds.

"Excuse me!" shouted Ben. "Can I have my ball back, please?"

"Here you are," said the old man, throwing the ball over the wall. "You've just moved in, haven't you?"

"Yes. We moved in yesterday. My name's Ben."

"Nice to meet you, Ben," said the old man. "My name's Mr Hopkins, but you can call me Jack."

"Do you work in your garden every day?" asked Ben.

"Come rain or shine," laughed Jack. "There's a lot to do here as you can see, and I'm a bit slower than I used to be."

Over the next few days, Ben and Jack got to know each other better. Ben liked listening to Jack talking about his garden, while Jack enjoyed listening to Ben talking about football.

Soon after, Jack invited Ben and his parents for tea in the summerhouse. They all agreed that Jack's was the best garden they had ever seen. Ben's mum couldn't believe that Jack knew the name of every single flower and bush.

That night, there was a dreadful storm. The rain lashed down, and the wind whistled around the houses for hours. In the morning, Ben went outside, and couldn't believe what he saw when he looked over the wall. Jack's garden was totally ruined! Many of the flowers and bushes had been uprooted. The windows of the summerhouse were broken, and the door had come off its hinges. Even the little bridge over the pond was smashed.

"Mum!" yelled Ben, running into the kitchen, "Have you seen what's happened to Jack's garden?"

"I know," said Mum quietly. "There was an awful storm while you were asleep last night. Jack tried to rescue his pot plants. Unfortunately, he tripped up and hurt his leg and had to be taken to hospital."

"Is he alright?" asked Ben.

"It's not serious," said Mum. "He'll be back in a few days. But it's very sad about his garden."

Ben felt miserable. Not only had
his new friend been hurt, but his beautiful
garden had been almost completely destroyed.
That night, Ben had an idea. He told his
parents that he'd like to try to fix Jack's garden
before he arrived back from hospital. They thought
it was a brilliant idea.
The next day, Ben started to clear up all the plants
that the storm had destroyed. Then his mother showed
him how to plant the new ones that she'd bought.

Ben worked hard over the next few days. While he and Mum carried on with the planting, Dad fixed the summerhouse. He completely rebuilt the little bridge that crossed the pond.

Finally the garden was finished, and Ben hoped that Jack would like what they'd done. When Jack came out of hospital and saw his magnificent new garden, his eyes filled with tears of joy.

"I can't believe you've done all this for me," he said.

"It was Ben's idea," said Mum proudly. "And he did most of the work."

"Ben, I can't thank you enough," said Jack gratefully.

Next Saturday, as Ben was getting ready to watch his football team play on television, Jack appeared at the front door. To Ben's amazement, Jack held up two tickets for the football match that afternoon.

"One for me, and one for you," twinkled the old man kindly.

"Wow!" said Ben excitedly. "I've never been to a real match before!"

"It's the least I can do after all the hard work you've done," said Jack.

Ben grabbed his jacket, and said goodbye to Mum and Dad. Then he and Jack walked hand in hand down the road together – to watch a *real* football match.

Milly's Magic Wand

Nick Ellsworth

*T*oday was Milly's birthday, and she had invited round her best friends for her birthday party.

After they had finished tea and had all eaten a slice of Milly's birthday cake, the children played some party games. Then, they sat down on the sitting-room floor to watch a magic show.

Everyone became very quiet when a tall man with white hair and a long, white beard came into the room. He was wearing a top hat and a big black cloak.

"Hello children!" he called out in a deep voice. "I am … the Great Salvini!", and in one quick move, he reached behind his ear and pulled out a beautiful red rose.

"This is going to be good," thought Milly.

The Great Salvini kept the children spellbound for a long time with his tricks. At one point he even pulled a rose from behind Milly's mum's ear!

But the Great Salvini saved his best trick of all until last.

He took off his top hat, and showed the children the inside so they could see it was empty. He then tapped it with his magic wand, and out popped a real white rabbit.

Milly gasped with astonishment. How could a real live rabbit come out of an empty hat? She went to bed that night trying to work it out.

The next morning, Milly and her mum went to the school jumble sale.

As she looked through a pile of old toys, out of the corner of one eye Milly spotted a shabby-looking box. It had a label "MAGIC SET" stuck on the front. Perhaps the box would hold the secret of how to pull a rabbit out of a hat!

Milly used some of her birthday money to buy the magic set, and then she and Mum set off home. As soon as they reached the house, Milly rushed up to her bedroom to look at her magic set.

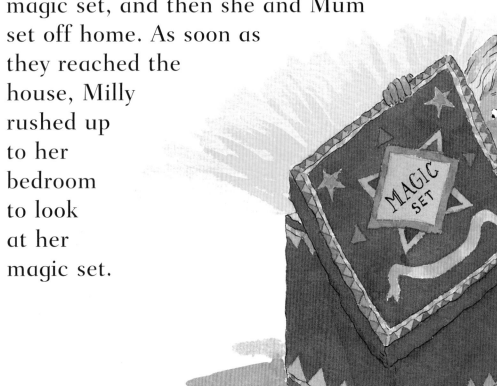

There were lots of tricks inside it, including a magic wand and a top hat. There was even a little book telling her how to do the tricks. But it didn't say anything about pulling a rabbit out of a hat.

Suddenly, Milly noticed a small flap at the bottom of the box. She pulled it, and found a secret drawer beneath the flap. Inside the drawer was a magnificent golden wand.

"I wonder if this will make a rabbit come out of the hat?" she thought.

Milly tapped the top hat with the golden wand, and waited to see if anything would happen. She could hardly believe it when, moments later, a real live rabbit poked its head out of the hat.

"I can do it! I can do it!" yelled Milly, jumping up and down. Picking up the rabbit, she ran downstairs to show her trick to Mum and Dad.

Startled by Milly's yelling, her younger brother Jack rushed into her room.

When he saw the gleaming golden wand, Jack picked it up. He began to bang it on the magic hat like a drum!

Suddenly, another rabbit popped out of the hat.

"Wow ... a rabbit!" cried Jack excitedly, banging on the hat even more. This made even more rabbits pop out!

Soon, there were rabbits all over Milly's bedroom. They were hopping on her bed, scrambling under her wardrobe and even munching on her pillow!

Hearing all the banging, Milly and her parents dashed into her bedroom to see what all the noise was about. When they saw the roomful of rabbits, they couldn't believe their eyes.

"Look at them all!" cried Dad. "Where have all these rabbits come from?"

"Out of the top hat, I think," said Milly.

"What are we going to do with them?" groaned Dad. "They can't stay here!"

"Of course they can't, poor things. We must set them free in the field," replied Mum.

So Milly, Mum
and Dad spent the rest of
the afternoon carrying the
rabbits into the field at the
back of the garden. And, one by
one, they set them all free.

Milly was sad to see all the rabbits go, but she knew
that it was the best thing to do.

The next day, Milly and her mum decided to take the
golden wand to the Great Salvini. It had far too much
magic in it to keep inside the house.

When he saw the golden wand, the old magician
almost fell off his chair with amazement.

"This wand has been missing for many years. It has great magical powers," he explained. "There are only five such wands in the whole world. Thank you so much for finding it. I will treasure it for ever."

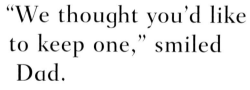

When Milly and Mum returned home, Dad told Milly to close her eyes. He put something warm and furry into Milly's hands.

Opening her eyes, Milly was thrilled to see that it was one of the rabbits.

"We thought you'd like to keep one," smiled Dad.

"Oh thanks, Dad! Thanks, Mum!" said Milly, with a large grin on her face. Holding her rabbit gently, she went up to her bedroom to give her new rabbit friend a very big hug.

Harrrum!

Tony Payne

Claire and Warren Brown lived with their parents in a small cottage on the edge of a sandy beach. The two children liked living there, and they liked their school too.

Yesterday, they had learned about dinosaurs at school. Their teacher, Miss Vinegar, had shown them photos of dinosaur eggs that were so old they had turned into stone.

The photos reminded Claire and Warren of something they had found on the beach the other day. It looked like a stone, but it was so perfectly smooth and round that they had taken it home. The next day, they took the stone into school to show Miss Vinegar.

"Is it a dinosaur egg?" they asked excitedly.

"Well now," said Miss Vinegar, sniffing. "I hardly think children would be able to find a real dinosaur egg. In fact it's just a big stone, that's all."

Disappointed, the two children took the stone back home and put it by the fire, where they could look at the lovely patterns all over it. There were long wiggly lines that looked like gold by the light of the fire. And the sparkling bits here and there could be diamonds!

When Claire and Warren went down to breakfast next morning, they had a big surprise. The 'stone' was cracking! They watched in amazement as a little scaly face pushed its way out of the shell, and stopped still when it saw them.

"Haa!" it said. "Humumm!"

"Mum!" shrieked Claire. "It's a baby dragon!"

"Very nice, dear," said Mum.

"A dragon, Mum!" cried Warren.

"Yes, dear, so you said," said Mum. "But there's no room in here for a dragon! I'm not having it dirtying my kitchen. You'll have to put it in your cave, out of the way."

The children had their own secret cave. The opening to it was in the garden, and no one else knew about it, apart from Mum.

"But what shall we feed it on?" asked Warren.

"I don't know," said Mum. "Celery?"

"Dragons don't eat celery!" said Warren.

"You'd best ask your father then," said Mum.

The children tried out everything in the fridge, and then the cupboards and the freezer. The little dragon liked dog food best. "Yum!" it said. It also liked celery.

"Told you!" said Mum.

Claire and Warren called their new pet Harrrum – because that was the sound it made. It would make a loud burp and then go 'harrrum!' as it coughed up horrible gases that smelled like stink-bombs.

The weeks passed and Harrrum grew quickly, eating almost anything it could get its claws on. It grew and it grew, and it seemed to think the children were its mum

and dad! Harrrum would grumble in delight when they stroked its long neck. It would gently push its face against the children's.

And then Harrrum grew wings!

More weeks and then months passed, and soon it was time for the school's Open Day. All the children were asked to bring in a pet, if they could. They had to stand up and tell the class what they would bring. Kathy Morris said she would bring Madge, her hamster. Sophie Atwood was going to ride to school on her pony, Tickles, and Graham Toogood said he'd bring in his best slug, Jelly!

"And what about you two?" asked Miss Vinegar, pointing at Claire and Warren. "What will you be bringing?"

"Please, Miss Vinegar," said Warren, as proud as can be. "We'll bring our pet dragon. His name is Harrrum."

"Did you say ... dragon?" asked their teacher. "Because if you did, that's not funny! There are no such things as dragons, as you well know. First it's dinosaurs, and now dragons. You are two very silly children!"

Miss Vinegar always seemed so cross.

On Open Day itself, Miss Vinegar stood on a low stage decorated with tissue-paper flowers and colourful streamers. It looked very jolly. Around the stage the children pushed or pulled all sorts of animals that didn't want to be pushed or pulled. Smaller creatures were being carried or were peeping out of pockets or, in the case of Jelly the slug, stuck to a glass jar.

Miss Vinegar showed the children old photographs of every cat she

had ever owned. "And this is Tiddles ... and this is Cuddle ... and here's Midge ... and this is Poppet." She'd had dozens of cats, and they all looked exactly the same. One picture would have done for the lot of them, and the children soon became bored.

Then Miss Vinegar noticed the class were not paying her any attention. They were looking up at the sky behind her. She turned ... and saw a dragon!

A six-metre-long dragon, with its huge wings spread out wide, was flying towards her. On its back sat Claire and Warren Brown, grinning and waving. A stunned Miss

Vinegar waved back feebly with just her fingers. Then, the dragon came in to land right beside Miss Vinegar.

"HARRRUM!!!" coughed the dragon, and a huge flame shot out of its long, toothy snout. This delighted the children … and frightened poor Miss Vinegar to bits. But Harrrum only pushed its big, scaly head gently against the teacher's face, just as it did with Claire and Warren. And then it gave Miss Vinegar a huge, wet, sloppy kiss!

The Pirate's Hat

Nick Ellsworth

Each summer, Patrick used to go and stay with his Uncle Max and Auntie Jess who lived in a tiny cottage by the sea.

One rainy afternoon, Patrick was indoors feeling a bit bored. Looking through Uncle Max's bookcase, he found a huge old book about pirates. Patrick settled into a comfy armchair, and began to read about one of the most dangerous pirates of all times, One-Armed Jake.

"I'm glad I'll never meet him," thought Patrick when he went to bed that night. "He's really scary!"

The next day was warm and sunny, and Patrick couldn't wait to go outdoors. He waved to Uncle Max and Auntie Jess, who were in the garden.

Then Patrick made his way down the steep, windy path to the beach.

After walking a little way along the sand, Patrick spotted a small gap in the cliff. He'd never noticed the gap before. It was the entrance to a small cave.

"It's very dark and cold in here," thought Patrick, as he stepped inside the cave. He shivered. "This feels a bit creepy."

Turning to leave, Patrick saw something half buried in the sand. He picked it up, and was amazed to see that it was an old and battered pirate's hat.

"Wow, a real pirate's hat!" cried Patrick, putting it on his head.

Suddenly, he began to feel very tired. He lay down on the sandy floor of the cave and fell asleep straightaway.

When he woke up, Patrick quickly realized that he was no longer in the cave. He was lying on the deck of a ship – in the middle of a huge battle! The roar of the cannon was deafening and, all around him, men were yelling and fighting with swords. They were pirates!

Patrick felt scared, and quickly hid behind a wooden barrel.

All of a sudden, a hand pulled Patrick out of his hiding-place. He found himself staring into the eyes of a pirate with only one arm.

"It's One-Armed Jake!" thought Patrick with horror.

"Come with me, lad. We've got work to do!" shouted One-Armed Jake fiercely, and he pushed Patrick roughly to the side of the ship.

Bobbing around in a small rowing boat in the sea below were two more pirates. Between them was a large wooden chest.

"Get in the rowing boat, lad. No funny tricks, mind! I'll be right behind you," snarled One-Armed Jake.

He pushed Patrick down a rope ladder and into the waiting boat. One-Armed Jake followed swiftly behind.

"Row, me shipmates, row!" yelled One-Armed Jake.

"Where are we going?" asked Patrick.

"To the beach to bury my money. See this chest, lad. My old enemy, Cap'n Saltwater, wants to steal it from me. That's what all the fighting's about!"

One-Armed Jake opened the box, and Patrick couldn't believe what he saw. Hundreds of gold coins lay glinting inside. From the corner of his eye, Patrick noticed a single

gold coin in the bottom of the
boat. He quickly picked it up and put it in his pocket,
hoping that none of the pirates had been watching.

When they arrived at the beach, Patrick and the
pirates dragged the heavy chest towards a nearby cave.
They dug a deep hole, dropped the chest into it, and
covered it over with sand.

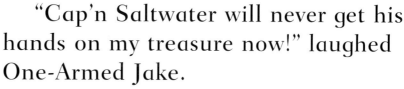

"Cap'n Saltwater will never get his hands on my treasure now!" laughed One-Armed Jake.

"What about the boy? He knows exactly where the treasure's hidden!" growled one pirate, who had a huge scar across one cheek. "He could tell anybody where it is, or even come back and steal it for himself."

"That's true," said One-Armed Jake, looking at Patrick with his cold eyes. "Maybe we should bury him with the treasure."

Now Patrick felt really frightened.

"But, before we do anything," continued One-Armed Jake, "the boy's got something of mine!"

"Oh, no!" thought Patrick. "He knows about the coin in my pocket." Patrick trembled. "I'm in for it now."

"The boy's got my favourite ... HAT!" roared One-Armed Jake, and grabbed it off Patrick's head.

At that moment, there was a huge flash, and Patrick closed his eyes. When he opened them again, the pirates were nowhere to be seen. Patrick was lying alone in the cave, with One-Armed Jake's hat by his side. Everything seemed to be back to normal again.

Patrick sat up and rubbed his eyes.

"What a scary dream," he thought. "And yet it seemed so real!"

Patrick picked up the hat and ran back up to the cottage to tell Uncle Max and Auntie Jess what had happened.

"How terrifying! I'm glad it was just a dream," said Uncle Max, after listening to Patrick's story during tea.

All of a sudden, something fell out of Patrick's pocket. When the three of them saw what it was, they all gasped with surprise.

There on the floor, glinting in the sunlight, lay a shiny, bright gold coin.

A Surprise for Lulu

Jan Payne

Lulu was the happiest little girl in the world. Her mum called her "Little Miss Smiley". Lulu especially loved being helpful.

"Lulu, will you feed Bonnie for me?" asked Miss Coxan from next door.

"Yes, Miss Coxan," answered Lulu. She loved feeding Miss Coxan's cat.

"Lulu, will you help me bath Bonzo?" asked Mr Felps from across the road.

"Yes, Mr Felps," answered Lulu.

Bonzo was a big, shaggy sheepdog. Bathing him was fun. Well Lulu thought so, but she wasn't sure that Bonzo did. It was odd, but when he heard the tin bath being filled with water in the garden, he always hid under the kitchen table.

"Come on, Bonzo," Lulu would call softly. "Look what I've got," she cooed, showing him the squeaky duck she had brought for him to play with. But Bonzo wouldn't move.

Together, Lulu and Mr Felps always had to lift Bonzo into the bath. He would stick out his legs stiffly in front of him, so they had to wait for him to bend them before they could get him in the water. Still, Bonzo got his own back afterwards. He would charge around the garden, shaking water everywhere while Lulu and Mr Felps ran for cover.

Whenever Grandma was really busy she would ask Lulu to clean out Twitch's hutch. Twitch was Grandma's rabbit. Lulu had named him because his nose was always twitching. She took the dirty straw out of the hutch and put clean straw back. Then she gave Twitch the lettuce she had bought with her own pocket money. The rabbit was so friendly that he would sit on Lulu's lap for hours while she stroked his soft silky fur.

Sometimes Farmer Booth asked Lulu to groom his carthorse Pickle. This was the best thing of all. Pickle was so big, but also so gentle. He stood perfectly still while Farmer Booth brushed one side, and Lulu brushed the other. Lulu had to stand on a box so that she could reach. Afterwards, she always gave Pickle a carrot.

Lulu's best friend was Laurence. He lived at Spring Farm, and whenever she could Lulu went over there to play. Laurence showed Lulu how to play conkers, and she showed him how to knit. Boys don't often knit but Laurence liked it. He and Lulu had competitions to see who could knit a scarf with the most colours. Once Laurence knitted a scarf that was all the colours of the rainbow. Lulu liked it so much that he gave it to her.

In three weeks' time it would be Lulu's sixth birthday. Mum said she could have a BIG party, and she could invite all her friends. Lulu was so excited she could hardly wait.

Then, a week before the party, Lulu's mum became ill.

"It's a nasty attack of flu," the doctor told her. "You need to stay in bed for a few days. I'm sure this young lady will help look after you," she added, smiling at Lulu.

"I'm so sorry, Lulu," said Mum, hugging her when the doctor had gone. "But you won't be able to have your party after all."

"I don't mind," said Lulu, turning away so that Mum couldn't see how disappointed she felt.

Grandma came to stay, and Lulu helped as much as she could. She didn't mention her party once, although she did think about it when she was on her own.

On the day of her birthday, Lulu went to school as usual. She did her lessons. She played with her friends. She ate her school dinner. It seemed just like any ordinary day. She couldn't help feeling a little bit sad.

In the afternoon, when the school bus dropped her on the village green, Lulu had the biggest surprise of her life!

The green had been decorated with fairy lights and balloons. There were tables and chairs on the grass. The tables were covered in white cloths, and there was a birthday cake and a pile of presents on one of them. Mr Felps had lit a barbecue and was cooking chicken and sausages on it. The smell was fantastic. There was

also a big, bright bouncy castle, and high in the air, between two trees, was a long banner that said:

HAPPY BIRTHDAY, Little Miss Smiley!

Everyone was there – Farmer Booth, Miss Coxan, Grandma, Laurence and all Lulu's friends from school. They had arranged everything secretly so that it would be a complete surprise for her. As they sang

"Happy birthday to you, happy birthday to you,
Happy birthday dear Lulu, happy birthday to you,"

Lulu thought it was the best moment of her life. It was even better still when Mum appeared, wrapped up in a big coat. She was feeling well enough to join in.

"What do you think?" she asked Lulu, giving her a big hug.

Lulu was so happy she couldn't speak. Her brilliant smile said it all!

"Happy birthday, little Miss Smiley!" said Mum.